Bowly Can CRUSH a Problem

A Grit & Resilience Story
by Angharad Davies

The Positive
Motherhood Project

First published in 2024 by The Positive Motherhood Project Ltd

www.bowlycan.com

© 2024 Angharad Davies

ISBN: 978-1-7390947-2-0

Hello there!

I can't seem to find my friend.
His name's Bowly McLight.
He's a little light-filled bowl.
We were supposed to meet up here.

Hold on.
I think I hear something.
It sounds a lot like puffing.
I wonder...

Here you are, Bowly!
Was that you doing all that puffing?
It looks like you were trying to blow
up that red balloon.

And I can see you have a stone
there blocking your light. A stone
normally comes when you're finding
something tough, doesn't it?

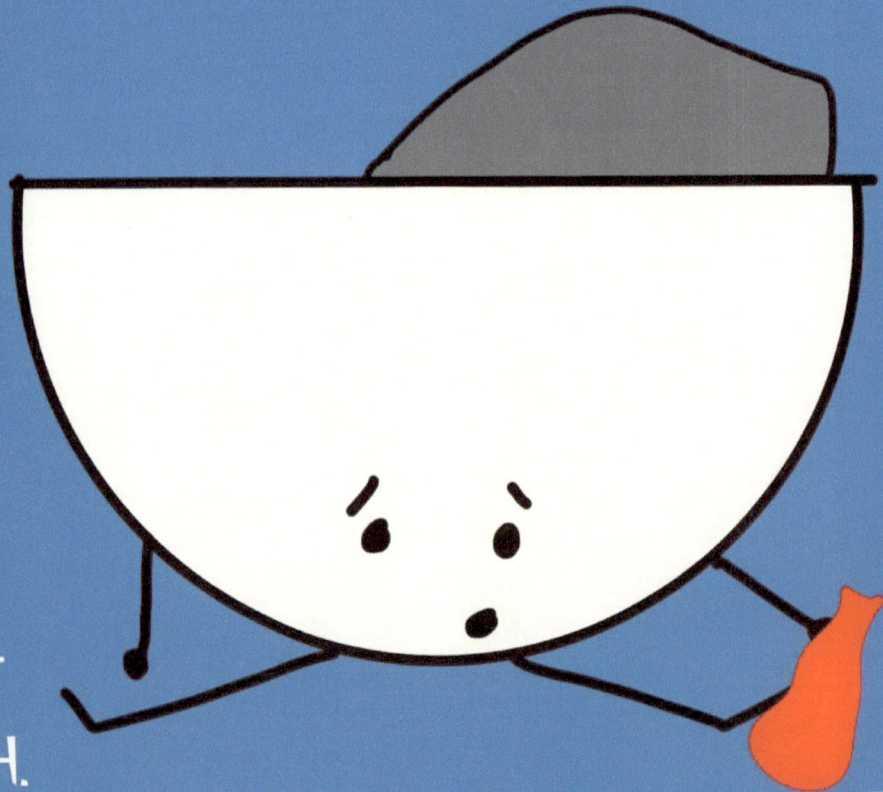

YEAH.

Hold on a second.
You're taking the stone out.
What are you going to do with it, Bowly?

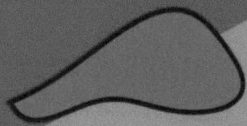

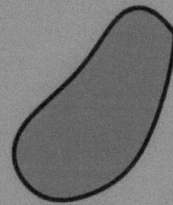

Wowee!
You've karate-chopped that stone into three.

And now you're looking closely at each part of the stone that was blocking your light.

Hmmm...
What's the hard part?
What's the hard part?

A pump! What a great idea to get more puff.
Wow, you blew up that balloon in lightning speed.
Look, Bowly! The stones have vanished and your
light is shining again.

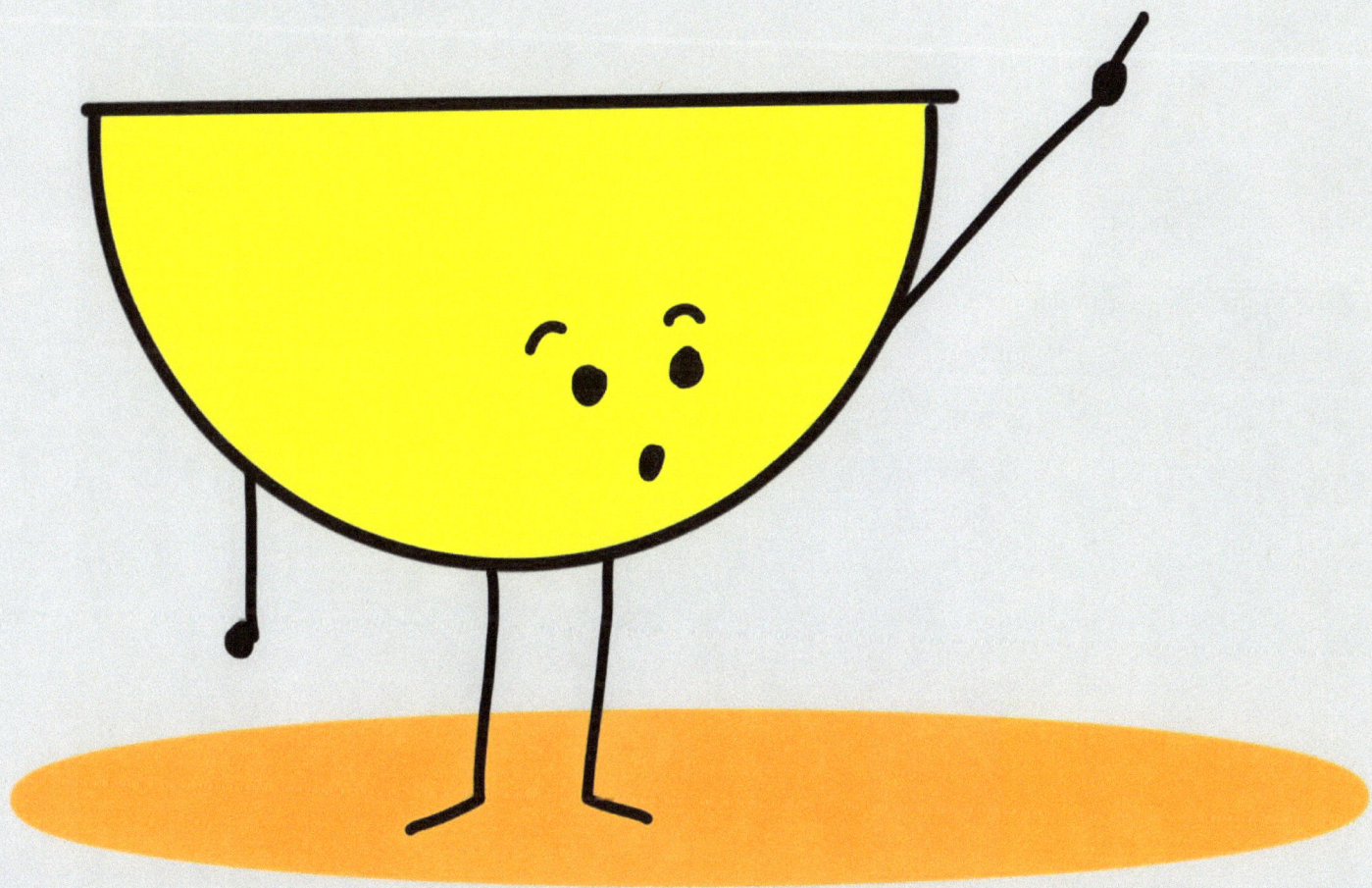

What is it, Bowly?
Have you spotted something?

Ah, you found a swimming pool.
Bowly, you look scared and a stone is blocking
your light again.
A stone normally blocks your light when
you feel frightened, doesn't it?
This stone looks bigger than the last one, too.
What are you going to do, Bowly?

Crikey! You've karate-chopped that stone into five pieces!

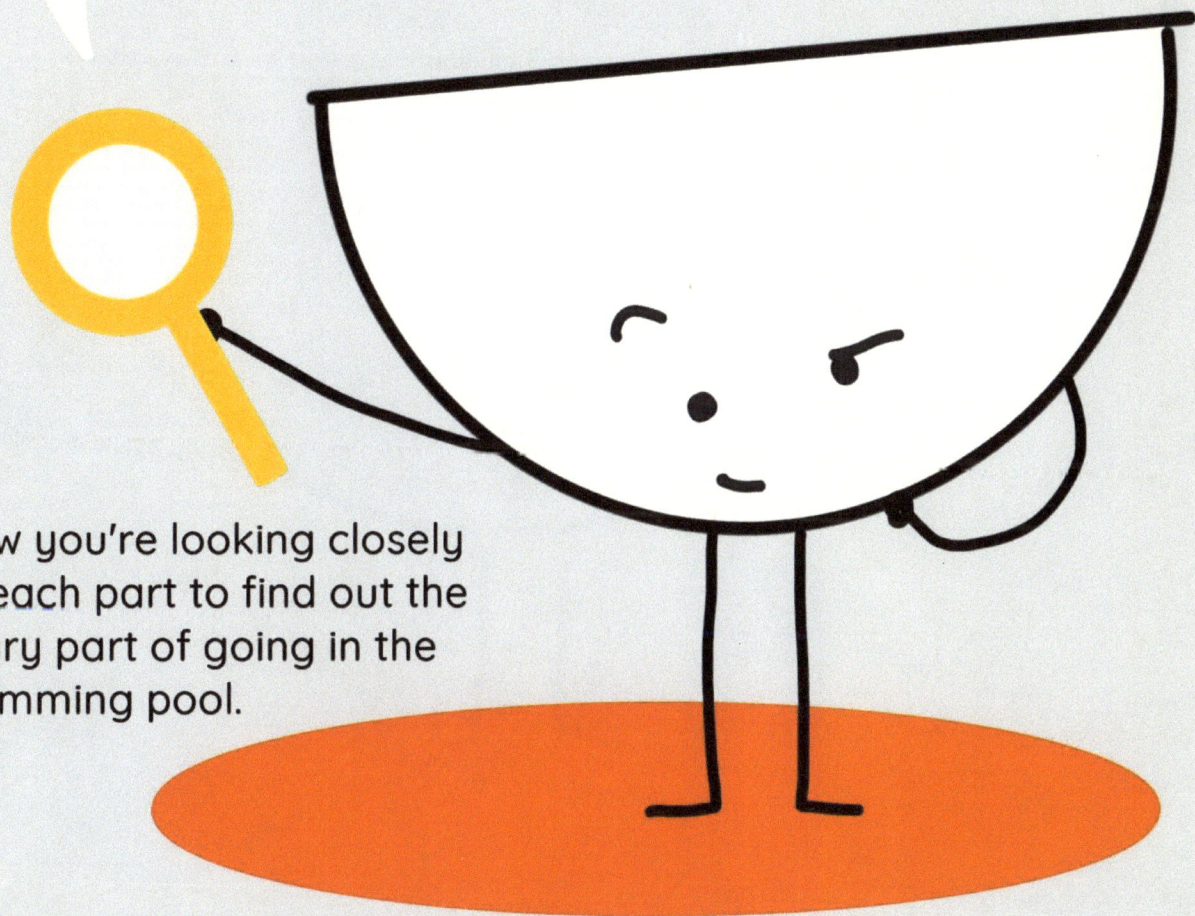

Hmm...
What's the scary part?
What's the scary part?

Now you're looking closely at each part to find out the scary part of going in the swimming pool.

Genius!
You're using balloons
to stay afloat.
Look, your light is
shining again.

Huh?

You've finished swimmimg already, Bowly. That was quick.
I see you've spotted something over there.
What do you think it could be?

Holy moly, Bowly!
Look at that dragon!
Look at that stone!
What are you going to do?

Wowzers! You've smashed that giant stone to smithereens.
There must be so many tough and scary parts to consider.

What's the hard part?
What's the scary part?

FIRE!!!

Balloons?!
I don't think balloons and a pump can help you this time, Bowly!

Or can they?
You're filling the balloon with water, not air.
It looks like you have a plan, Bowly.
I wonder...

Kablooie!

You put out the fire with the water balloon, Bowly!
Your light is shining once again.
That'll be the last we see of that dragon.
Come on, Bowly. It's time to go home.

The story might be over, but Bowly has one last thing for you.

Make Bowly's tool come alive in the FREE video training

Take your very own Bowly with you wherever you go!
Learn how to use the super-duper-problem-solving karate chop at home, at school and out and about.

If Bowly can...

... so can you!

www.bowlycan.com/f/chop

About the author

Angharad Davies lives in the UK with her ever-so-supportive husband and her two amazing little boys.

After witnessing the magic of story in her own children for nurturing emotional intelligence and resilience, she decided to write her own.

Combining her knowledge from postgraduate qualifications in Psychology and Play Therapy with her children's love for humorous reads, Bowly McLight was born. With the help of her own children's story ideas and illustrations, Angharad is on a mission to deliver practical mindset and resilience tools to children through the power of story.

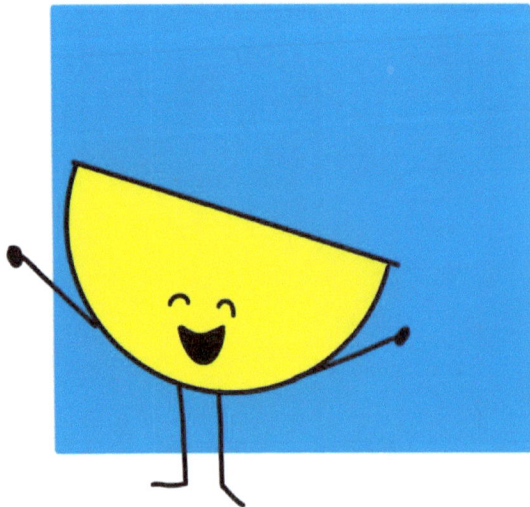

About Bowly

Bowly was inspired by the Hawaiian teaching of the Bowl of Light.

He is fun-loving and adores a challenge. He wears his big emotions on his sleeve and is on a mission to teach children everywhere the coolest of tools, so that they too can face anything life throws at them - even big dragons!

A new tool in every story

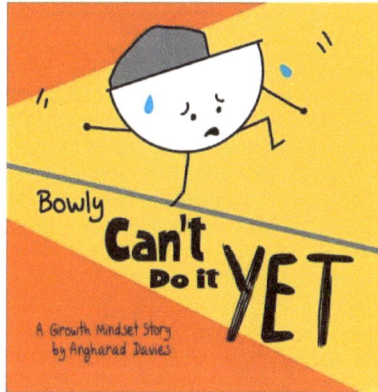

Bowly is frustrated and ready to give up learning to walk the tightrope when a mysterious word appears. Where did it come from and can it help Bowly to keep going?

A charming story to introduce children to the power of *yet* and learning to persevere when things get tough. The perfect book for helping children to build resilience and growth mindset.

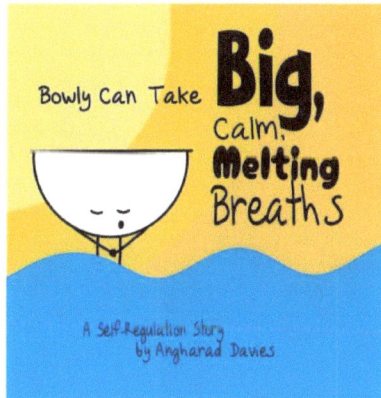

Bowly is covered in mud and feeling angry, but he has just the right tool: his big, calm, melting breath. There is just a bit more melting than he had anticipated!

A fun story to introduce children to a practical and powerful breathing tool. The perfect book for nurturing self-regulation and mindfulness.

www.ingramcontent.com/pod-product-compliance
Lightning Source LLC
LaVergne TN
LVHW072108070426
835509LV00002B/75